MINDFUL LEADERSHIP IN THE ARTS

BALANCING CREATIVITY, WELL-BEING, AND PERFORMANCE

DENISE ZUBIZARRETA

© Denise Zubizarreta

Denise Zubizarreta
LEAP Institute for the Arts
Arts Leadership & Cultural Management
Colorado State University

For Mom.

TABLE OF CONTENTS

Prologue — 8

Chapter 1 — 9

Understanding Mindful Leadership in the Arts — 9

What is Mindful Leadership? — 9

Key Principles of Mindful Leadership in the Arts: — 10

The Role of Emotional Intelligence (EQ) — 10

Mindfulness in Action — 12

Why Mindfulness Matters in the Arts — 12

Practical Exercises for Incorporating Mindfulness into Daily Routines — 13

Mindful Breathing — 13

Body Scans — 14

Reflective Journaling — 14

Mindful Listening — 15

Mindful Walking — 15

Compassion Meditation — 15

Cultivating a Mindful Mindset in Leadership — 16

Embracing Mindful Leadership in the Arts — 17

Chapter 2 — 19

The Power of Self-Care for Arts Leaders — 19

Why Self-Care Matters — 19
Identifying and Overcoming Burnout — 20
Building Resilience Through Self-Care Practices — 23
Modeling Self-Care for Your Team — 25
Embracing Self-Care as a Leadership Strength — 26

Chapter 3 — 27

Mindfulness Techniques for Creative Leadership — 27

Meditation and Reflection Practices — 27
Guided Meditation for Leaders — 28
Reflective Practices for Insight and Innovation — 29
Prompts and Exercises for Meaningful Reflection — 31
Harnessing the Power of Mindfulness for Creative Leadership — 33

Chapter 4 — 34

Fostering a Mindful and Creative Team Culture — 34

Creating a Culture of Mindfulness and Well-being — 34
Encouraging Mindfulness in the Workplace — 34
Promoting Work-Life Balance — 36
Building Emotional Resilience in Teams — 38

Creating a Lasting Impact Through Mindful and Creative Team Culture   39

Chapter 5   41

The Impact of Mindful Leadership on Performance   41

Balancing Creativity and Performance   41

Enhancing Decision-Making and Problem-Solving   42

Boosting Creativity and Innovation   43

Improving Communication and Collaboration   44

The Ripple Effect of Mindful Leadership on Organizational Performance   46

Leading with Mindfulness for Peak Performance   47

Chapter 6   49

Integrating Mindfulness into Organizational Strategy   49

Mindfulness as a Strategic Priority   49

Embedding Mindfulness in Mission and Vision Statements   50

Mindful Strategic Planning   51

Creating Mindful Policies and Practices   52

Measuring the Impact of Mindfulness   53

Sustaining a Mindful Organization   55

Building a Mindful Organization for the Future   56

About the Author   **58**

PROLOGUE

Leadership in the arts is both a privilege and a challenge. Arts leaders are tasked with guiding creative vision, managing diverse teams, and ensuring the sustainability of their organizations—all while navigating the unique pressures and complexities that come with a creative environment. In such a dynamic and often unpredictable landscape, maintaining a sense of balance, clarity, and purpose is essential.

Mindful Leadership in the Arts addresses the importance of mindfulness and self-care for arts leaders, providing practical tools and strategies to enhance emotional intelligence, foster resilience, and support personal and professional well-being. This book explores how mindfulness practices—like meditation, deep listening, and conscious reflection—can help arts leaders navigate the complexities of their roles, inspire their teams, and create environments where creativity and performance can thrive.

CHAPTER 1

UNDERSTANDING MINDFUL LEADERSHIP IN THE ARTS

What is Mindful Leadership?

Mindful leadership is about more than just managing tasks, setting goals, or steering an organization toward financial success. It is a holistic approach to leadership that emphasizes being fully present, aware, and intentional in every aspect of your role. As a mindful leader, you strive to make conscious choices that are deeply aligned with your values and those of your organization. You cultivate an environment where empathy, openness, creativity, and well-being flourish.

Mindful leadership is about leading with intention, compassion, and self-awareness. It requires a deep understanding of oneself and a genuine commitment to personal growth and the well-being of others. In the arts, where creativity and innovation are paramount, mindful leadership helps to build a culture that supports artistic expression while promoting mental and emotional resilience.

Key Principles of Mindful Leadership in the Arts:

> Presence: Being fully engaged in the present moment, whether in meetings, creative discussions, or during moments of reflection.
>
> Compassion: Approaching interactions with kindness, understanding, and empathy, and recognizing the unique contributions and needs of each team member.
>
> Intention: Leading with clarity and purpose, ensuring that decisions align with both personal and organizational values.
>
> Authenticity: Being genuine and transparent in all communications and actions, fostering trust and openness within the team.

The Role of Emotional Intelligence (EQ)

Emotional intelligence (EQ) is a foundational element of mindful leadership. EQ involves the capacity to recognize, understand, and manage one's own emotions, as well as the emotions of others. In the context of arts leadership, high EQ is crucial for fostering a culture that is both creatively vibrant and emotionally supportive.

There are four key components of EQ that are particularly relevant for arts leaders:

Self-Awareness: Self-awareness is the ability to understand your own emotions, strengths, weaknesses, and values, and how they affect your behavior and decisions. For arts leaders, self-awareness means being conscious of how your emotions influence your interactions with your team and your responses to challenges. It involves regular self-reflection to recognize your emotional triggers, biases, and habits, allowing you to lead more effectively and authentically.

Self-Regulation: Self-regulation is the ability to manage your emotions, especially in stressful or challenging situations. It involves staying calm, maintaining self-control, and reacting thoughtfully rather than impulsively. For arts leaders, self-regulation is vital when dealing with the pressures of tight deadlines, conflicting opinions, or creative tensions. It enables you to respond to challenges with resilience and adaptability, creating a stable environment for your team.

Social Awareness: Social awareness is the ability to understand the emotions, needs, and concerns of others. It involves empathy—recognizing and valuing the perspectives of your team members, artists, audiences, and stakeholders. For arts leaders, social awareness helps in navigating diverse viewpoints, fostering inclusivity, and creating a supportive, collaborative environment. It allows you to connect with others on a deeper level, building trust and respect across your organization.

<u>Relationship Management</u>: Relationship management is the ability to build and maintain healthy, productive relationships. It involves effective communication, conflict resolution, and inspiring and motivating others. In the arts, where collaboration is often key to success, relationship management is essential for cultivating a team culture where creative ideas can be shared openly, conflicts are resolved constructively, and every member feels valued and heard.

By developing and enhancing these components of EQ, arts leaders can create a more compassionate, creative, and resilient organizational culture. High EQ enables leaders to navigate the emotional complexities of their role with grace and effectiveness, inspiring others to do the same.

Mindfulness in Action

Mindfulness, at its core, is the practice of being fully present in the moment without judgment. It involves paying attention to your thoughts, emotions, and sensations with a sense of openness and curiosity. For arts leaders, mindfulness means approaching decisions, challenges, and interactions with a calm, focused, and open mindset.

Why Mindfulness Matters in the Arts

In the fast-paced, high-pressure environment of the arts, mindfulness offers a way to pause, breathe, and reset. It allows leaders to step back from reactive tendencies, consider multiple perspectives, and respond thoughtfully rather than impulsively. Mindfulness fosters greater awareness, creativity, and clarity, enabling leaders to make decisions that are more aligned with their values and the needs of their organization.

Mindfulness also helps to create a positive work environment where team members feel heard, supported, and empowered. When leaders practice mindfulness, they model a way of being that encourages others to do the same. This modeling creates a ripple effect throughout the organization, promoting a culture where mindfulness, presence, and self-care become shared values. This kind of environment is especially important in the arts, where creativity thrives on emotional openness, trust, and a sense of psychological safety.

Practical Exercises for Incorporating Mindfulness into Daily Routines

To bring mindfulness into your leadership practice, consider incorporating the following exercises into your daily routine. These practices are designed to help you stay grounded, focused, and present, even amidst the busyness and unpredictability of arts leadership.

Mindful Breathing

One of the simplest yet most effective mindfulness practices is mindful breathing. Take a few moments each day to focus solely on your breath. Breathe in deeply through your nose, hold for a count of three, and then exhale slowly through your mouth. Notice the sensation of the air entering and leaving your body, and allow yourself to relax with each breath. Mindful breathing helps reduce stress, increases focus, and can be practiced anywhere—before a meeting, during a break, or at the start of your day.

Body Scans

A body scan is a mindfulness exercise that involves paying attention to the sensations in each part of your body, from your toes to your head. This practice helps you become more aware of any tension or discomfort you may be holding and encourages relaxation. To perform a body scan, find a quiet place to sit or lie down. Close your eyes and take a few deep breaths. Start by focusing on your toes, noticing any sensations you feel, and gradually move up through each part of your body—your legs, abdomen, chest, arms, and head. As you move through each area, breathe into any tension or tightness, allowing it to release with each exhale.

Reflective Journaling

Journaling can be a powerful tool for self-reflection and emotional processing. Set aside a few minutes each day to write about your experiences, thoughts, and emotions. Reflect on what went well, what challenged you, and what you learned. Ask yourself questions like, "What am I feeling right now?" "How did I handle today's challenges?" or "What can I do differently tomorrow?" Journaling helps you gain insight into your emotional patterns, clarify your thoughts, and set intentions for mindful growth.

Mindful Listening

Practice mindful listening during meetings, conversations, or even casual interactions. Focus entirely on the speaker, without interrupting or planning your response while they are talking. Notice the content of their words, their tone of voice, and their body language. Reflect back what you hear to ensure understanding and show that you value their perspective. Mindful listening fosters deeper connections, reduces misunderstandings, and builds trust within your team.

Mindful Walking

Integrate mindfulness into your daily routine through mindful walking. As you walk, focus on the sensation of your feet touching the ground, the rhythm of your steps, and the sights and sounds around you. Pay attention to your surroundings without rushing or distraction. Mindful walking can be a refreshing way to clear your mind, reduce stress, and gain a new perspective.

Compassion Meditation

Compassion meditation, or loving-kindness meditation, involves silently repeating phrases of goodwill, such as "May

I be happy, may I be healthy, may I be safe." You can extend these wishes to others—your team, your community, or people you find challenging. This practice fosters empathy, compassion, and emotional resilience, helping you approach leadership challenges with greater patience and understanding.

Cultivating a Mindful Mindset in Leadership

Mindfulness is not only a set of practices but also a mindset that can transform the way you lead. Cultivating a mindful mindset involves embracing principles of patience, acceptance, and non-judgment. It means being open to uncertainty, learning from every experience, and finding balance between striving for excellence and embracing imperfection.

> <u>Approach Challenges with Curiosity</u>: Instead of seeing challenges or conflicts as obstacles, view them as opportunities for learning and growth. Ask yourself, "What can I learn from this?" or "How can I grow from this experience?" This mindset shift helps you remain open to new possibilities and solutions, reducing stress and enhancing creativity.
>
> <u>Practice Self-Compassion</u>: Leadership can be demanding, and it's easy to become overly self-critical when things don't go as planned. Practice self-compassion by treating yourself with the same kindness and understanding that you would offer to a friend. Acknowledge your efforts, accept your

imperfections, and recognize that mistakes are part of the learning process.

Set Intentions for Each Day: Begin each day by setting a mindful intention. This could be an intention to stay present during meetings, to listen deeply, or to approach challenges with patience and creativity. Setting intentions helps anchor your actions in your values and brings clarity and purpose to your daily leadership practice.

Embracing Mindful Leadership in the Arts

Mindful leadership is about leading with presence, compassion, and purpose. It is about fostering an environment where creativity and well-being coexist, where leaders and teams can thrive. As an arts leader, embracing mindfulness can transform not only how you lead but also the culture of your organization. By integrating mindfulness into your daily routines and leadership practices, you can create a space where innovation, collaboration, and emotional intelligence flourish—paving the way for a more balanced, fulfilling, and impactful approach to leadership in the arts.

The journey to mindful leadership begins with small, intentional steps. Start today by incorporating a few mindfulness practices into your routine, and observe how they shape your interactions, decisions, and overall sense of well-being. As you continue to practice, you will find yourself more present, more resilient, and more connected to the creative potential of your team and organization.

CHAPTER 2

THE POWER OF SELF-CARE FOR ARTS LEADERS

Why Self-Care Matters

In the arts, where passion and creativity are deeply intertwined with professional responsibilities, self-care is often overlooked. Many arts leaders operate under the assumption that their commitment to the mission and their drive to achieve creative excellence require constant dedication and sacrifice. However, this mindset can lead to a cycle of overwork, stress, and eventual burnout. Self-care is not a luxury or an indulgence; it is an essential component of effective, sustainable leadership.

Arts leaders frequently juggle multiple roles, from crafting creative vision and managing diverse teams to overseeing fundraising efforts and engaging with community stakeholders. This continuous balancing act can quickly lead to feelings of overwhelm and exhaustion, ultimately affecting both personal well-being and organizational performance. Prioritizing self-care enables leaders to maintain their physical, emotional, and mental health, enhancing their capacity to make sound decisions, inspire their teams, and achieve long-term goals.

> The Impact of Neglecting Self-Care: When self-care is neglected, arts leaders may experience a range of negative outcomes, including decreased productivity, impaired decision-making, strained relationships, and a diminished ability to lead effectively. Chronic stress can weaken the immune system, increase the risk of anxiety and depression, and reduce overall job satisfaction. By prioritizing self-care, leaders can prevent these negative effects, foster greater resilience, and model healthy behaviors for their teams.

Identifying and Overcoming Burnout

Burnout is a state of physical, emotional, and mental exhaustion caused by prolonged and excessive stress. It often results from feeling overwhelmed, emotionally drained, and unable to meet constant demands. For arts leaders, burnout can manifest in various ways, such as loss of passion for the work, decreased productivity, increased irritability, and feelings of helplessness or detachment.

> Recognizing the Signs and Symptoms of Burnout: Early signs of burnout can include chronic fatigue, insomnia, difficulty concentrating, frequent headaches or muscle pain, and feelings of cynicism or detachment. Emotional symptoms might involve a sense of failure, self-doubt, and a pervasive feeling of

being overwhelmed. Behavioral signs can include withdrawing from responsibilities, isolating from colleagues, procrastinating, or neglecting personal care.

Emotional Symptoms: Feelings of cynicism, frustration, and helplessness. You may notice a loss of motivation, a sense of disconnection from your team or the mission, and an increased tendency to view work as a source of frustration rather than fulfillment.

Physical Symptoms: Chronic fatigue, headaches, muscle tension, or digestive problems. You might find yourself feeling physically drained at the end of the day, even when your work is primarily mental or emotional.

Behavioral Symptoms: Changes in behavior, such as withdrawal from responsibilities, procrastination, or increased irritability. You may notice that you are more likely to snap at colleagues, avoid challenging tasks, or disengage from conversations and meetings.

Strategies for Preventing and Overcoming Burnout: To prevent and address burnout, arts leaders need to implement proactive strategies that prioritize self-care and balance. Here are some key approaches:

Setting Boundaries: Establish clear boundaries between work and personal life to prevent overextension. This might involve setting specific work hours, creating a designated workspace, and making time for hobbies, family, and relaxation. Communicate these boundaries to your team and stakeholders, and respect them yourself to model healthy behavior.

Delegating Tasks: Effective delegation is essential for avoiding burnout. Trust your team by delegating responsibilities and tasks that align with their strengths and skills. This not only lightens your workload but also empowers your team, fosters professional development, and encourages a culture of collaboration and mutual support.

Prioritizing Rest and Recovery: Rest is a crucial component of self-care that often gets overlooked. Ensure you are getting sufficient sleep, taking regular breaks throughout the day, and scheduling time off to recharge. Incorporate micro-breaks into your workday to prevent mental fatigue, such as stretching, walking, or practicing deep breathing.

Mindful Time Management: Practice mindful time management by prioritizing tasks that align with your goals and values. Use tools like time-blocking, task lists, and project management software to organize your workload effectively. Avoid multitasking, as it can lead to decreased focus and increased stress.

Building Resilience Through Self-Care Practices

Resilience is the ability to bounce back from adversity, adapt to change, and maintain a sense of well-being amidst challenges. Building resilience is critical for arts leaders who face constant pressure to innovate, adapt, and lead through uncertainty. Self-care practices are key to developing resilience and maintaining a balanced, healthy approach to leadership.

> Regular Exercise: Physical activity is a proven way to reduce stress, boost mood, and increase energy levels. Incorporate regular exercise into your routine, whether it's a daily walk, a yoga session, or a dance class. Find activities that you enjoy and that fit into your schedule. Exercise not only improves physical health but also enhances mental clarity and emotional well-being.
>
> Balanced Nutrition: Nutrition plays a crucial role in overall well-being. Aim for a balanced diet that includes a variety of fruits, vegetables, whole grains, lean proteins, and healthy fats. Stay hydrated and avoid excessive caffeine or sugar, which can lead to energy crashes and mood swings. Nourishing your body with the right nutrients supports sustained energy, concentration, and a positive mood.
>
> Sufficient Sleep: Sleep is essential for cognitive function, emotional regulation, and physical health. Aim for 7-9 hours of quality sleep each night.

Establish a bedtime routine that promotes relaxation, such as turning off screens an hour before bed, reading, or practicing gentle stretching. Create a sleep environment that is cool, dark, and quiet to encourage restful sleep.

Relaxation Techniques: Incorporate relaxation techniques into your daily routine to reduce stress and enhance emotional resilience. Techniques such as meditation, deep breathing, progressive muscle relaxation, and mindfulness practices can help calm the mind and body, improve focus, and reduce anxiety. Experiment with different relaxation methods to find what works best for you.

Creating a Personalized Self-Care Plan: Every leader's self-care needs are unique, based on their personal preferences, lifestyle, and responsibilities. Develop a personalized self-care plan that includes activities and practices that nurture your physical, emotional, and mental well-being. Consider factors such as your daily schedule, personal interests, and energy levels when designing your plan.

Set Realistic Goals: Start small and set achievable goals for your self-care routine. For example, commit to a 10-minute mindfulness practice each morning or a 30-minute walk three times a week. Gradually increase the intensity or duration of your activities as they become habits.

> Schedule Self-Care Activities: Treat self-care as a priority by scheduling it into your calendar, just like you would for any other important meeting or task. Set aside dedicated time for exercise, relaxation, hobbies, or social activities, and protect that time from interruptions.

> Monitor and Adjust: Regularly assess your self-care practices to see what is working and what needs adjustment. Be flexible and willing to try new approaches if your current routine isn't meeting your needs. Listen to your body and mind, and make changes as necessary to support your overall well-being.

Modeling Self-Care for Your Team

As a leader, your actions set the tone for the entire organization. By prioritizing self-care and modeling healthy behaviors, you encourage your team to do the same. Foster a culture of well-being by promoting self-care practices and creating an environment where employees feel supported in managing their work-life balance.

> Encourage Open Conversations About Well-Being: Create a safe space for team members to discuss their well-being, share their experiences, and seek support. Lead by example by sharing your own self-care practices and experiences with burnout or stress management. Encourage a culture where self-care is viewed as a strength, not a weakness.

Support Flexibility and Work-Life Balance: Offer flexible work arrangements, such as remote work options or flexible hours, to help employees balance their personal and professional lives. Recognize that each team member's needs are different, and be open to accommodating their unique circumstances.

Promote Organizational Wellness Initiatives: Consider implementing wellness initiatives, such as mindfulness workshops, yoga classes, mental health days, or regular breaks during the workday. Provide resources for stress management, mental health support, and self-care practices. Celebrate wellness achievements and recognize team members who actively contribute to a culture of well-being.

Embracing Self-Care as a Leadership Strength

Self-care is a fundamental aspect of mindful leadership in the arts. By prioritizing your well-being, you enhance your ability to lead with clarity, compassion, and resilience. Self-care is not a sign of weakness but a demonstration of strength, self-awareness, and commitment to both personal and organizational health.

As you embrace self-care, you not only improve your own capacity for effective leadership but also inspire your team to do the same, creating a culture where creativity, well-being, and performance can thrive. Remember, a leader who cares for themselves is better equipped to care for others and to lead with vision, purpose, and vitality.

CHAPTER 3

MINDFULNESS TECHNIQUES FOR CREATIVE LEADERSHIP

Meditation and Reflection Practices

Mindfulness techniques such as meditation and reflection are essential tools for arts leaders who want to foster creativity, stay focused, and navigate the challenges of their roles with clarity and calm. These practices help leaders cultivate a deeper sense of presence, self-awareness, and emotional regulation, all of which are crucial for effective decision-making and creative thinking. In the fast-paced, high-pressure environment of the arts, where inspiration must often strike amid chaos, mindfulness practices offer a way to reset, refresh, and renew the mind.

This chapter explores various mindfulness techniques that arts leaders can use to enhance their creativity, decision-making, and overall well-being. From guided meditation to reflective practices, these tools will help you stay grounded and inspired, allowing you to lead with greater authenticity and effectiveness.

Guided Meditation for Leaders

Guided meditation is a practice in which a leader is led by a facilitator or recorded voice to focus their mind and cultivate mindfulness. This technique can help calm the mind, reduce stress, and enhance clarity and decision-making by promoting relaxation and focused awareness. Different types of meditation can be tailored to the specific needs of an arts leader, providing various benefits for creativity, leadership, and emotional balance.

> Focused Attention Meditation: This form of meditation involves concentrating on a single point of focus, such as the breath, a sound, or a visual object. For arts leaders, focused attention meditation can help train the mind to maintain concentration amid distractions, fostering greater mental clarity and discipline. By regularly practicing focused attention, leaders can improve their ability to stay present and focused in meetings, creative sessions, and decision-making processes.
>
> Loving-Kindness Meditation (Metta Meditation): Loving-kindness meditation involves silently repeating phrases of goodwill and compassion, first directed toward oneself and then extended to others, including colleagues, collaborators, and even those with whom one may have conflicts. This practice helps cultivate empathy, compassion, and emotional resilience, which are critical qualities for arts leaders who must navigate diverse perspectives, manage

conflicts, and build cohesive teams. Loving-kindness meditation can foster a more compassionate and supportive leadership style, promoting a positive organizational culture.

Body Scan Meditation: Body scan meditation is a mindfulness practice that involves paying attention to different parts of the body, moving from head to toe, and noticing any sensations or areas of tension. This practice can help leaders become more attuned to their bodies, recognizing early signs of stress or fatigue. By practicing body scan meditation regularly, arts leaders can develop greater self-awareness and learn to release physical tension, which can improve overall well-being and reduce the risk of burnout.

How to Integrate Meditation into Your Daily Routine: Start by dedicating a few minutes each day to meditation. Choose a quiet space where you won't be interrupted, and set a timer for five to ten minutes to begin with. Gradually increase the length of your sessions as you become more comfortable with the practice. Consider using guided meditation apps or online resources to help you get started. Make meditation a regular part of your daily routine, such as in the morning to set the tone for the day, during a lunch break to reset, or in the evening to unwind.

Reflective Practices for Insight and Innovation

Reflection is a powerful tool for self-exploration, creativity, and personal growth. For arts leaders, reflective practices offer opportunities to gain insight into their thoughts, emotions, and behaviors, fostering a deeper understanding of themselves and their leadership style. Reflection also encourages creative thinking, problem-solving, and innovation by allowing leaders to pause, consider multiple perspectives, and explore new ideas.

> Journaling: Journaling is a reflective practice that involves writing down your thoughts, feelings, experiences, and insights. For arts leaders, journaling can serve as a tool for processing emotions, clarifying thoughts, and setting intentions. Use prompts such as "What did I learn today?" "What challenges did I face?" or "How did I respond to a difficult situation?" to guide your reflections. Regular journaling can help you track your growth, identify patterns, and uncover new ideas, ultimately enhancing your leadership practice.
>
> Mindful Walking: Mindful walking is a practice that involves walking slowly and deliberately, paying attention to the sensations of your feet on the ground, your breath, and the sights and sounds around you. This practice can help clear the mind, reduce stress, and promote creative thinking. For arts leaders, mindful walking can be particularly useful during breaks between meetings or when seeking inspiration. Take a few minutes to walk outside, focusing on the present moment and letting go of

any distractions. Notice how the practice helps you return to your work with renewed energy and perspective.

Deep Listening: Deep listening is a practice of fully attending to another person without judgment, distraction, or the intention to respond immediately. For arts leaders, deep listening fosters empathy, trust, and connection with team members, collaborators, and stakeholders. Practice deep listening by giving your full attention to the speaker, maintaining eye contact, and focusing on their words, tone, and body language. Resist the urge to interrupt or formulate a response while they are speaking. Reflect back what you have heard to ensure understanding and show that you value their perspective.

Prompts and Exercises for Meaningful Reflection

To help arts leaders engage in meaningful reflection, here are several prompts and exercises designed to enhance self-awareness, creativity, and leadership skills:

Daily Reflection Prompt: At the end of each day, take a few minutes to reflect on the following questions:

- What was the most meaningful experience I had today, and why?
- How did I handle a challenge or difficult situation?
- What emotions did I experience, and how did I respond to them?

- What am I grateful for today?

Use these reflections to identify areas of growth, celebrate successes, and set intentions for the following day.

Creative Problem-Solving Exercise: When faced with a creative block or a complex challenge, try this exercise:

- Find a quiet space and take a few deep breaths to center yourself.
- Write down the challenge or problem you are facing in a few sentences.
- Close your eyes and visualize different possible solutions, without judging or dismissing any ideas.
- Open your eyes and jot down all the ideas that came to mind, no matter how unconventional or far-fetched.
- Review your list and identify one or two ideas that seem most promising or inspiring. Consider how you might explore or implement these ideas further.

Mindful Leadership Reflection: Use this exercise to deepen your understanding of your leadership style and goals:

- Take a moment to reflect on your values as a leader. What principles guide your decisions and actions?
- Think about a recent leadership challenge you faced. How did your values influence your response?
- Consider how you can align your daily actions more closely with your values. What changes might you need to make?

- Reflect on how mindfulness could enhance your leadership practice. How might you integrate mindfulness more fully into your daily routine?

Harnessing the Power of Mindfulness for Creative Leadership

Mindfulness techniques like meditation and reflection are not only tools for personal well-being but also powerful catalysts for creative leadership. By incorporating these practices into your daily routine, you can cultivate a calm, focused, and innovative mindset that enhances your ability to lead with authenticity, empathy, and vision.

Mindfulness allows you to stay present and engaged, even in challenging situations, and helps you respond to difficulties with clarity and grace. It opens up new pathways for creative thinking, encouraging you to explore fresh ideas, approach problems from different angles, and connect more deeply with your team and community.

By committing to mindfulness practices, you will find yourself better equipped to navigate the complexities of leadership in the arts, fostering a culture of creativity, collaboration, and well-being that supports your organization's mission and goals. Embrace these techniques as part of your journey toward mindful leadership, and watch as they transform not only how you lead but also how your organization thrives.

CHAPTER 4

FOSTERING A MINDFUL AND CREATIVE TEAM CULTURE

Creating a Culture of Mindfulness and Well-being

Arts leaders have a unique opportunity to shape the culture of their organizations in ways that support both individual well-being and collective creativity. By fostering a mindful and compassionate culture, leaders can create an environment where every team member feels valued, respected, and empowered to contribute their best work. A mindful culture promotes collaboration, innovation, and resilience, enabling the entire organization to thrive.

This chapter explores how arts leaders can cultivate a culture of mindfulness and well-being, emphasizing the importance of mindfulness in the workplace, promoting a healthy work-life balance, and building emotional resilience within teams. These strategies will help create an atmosphere where creativity and collaboration are nurtured, and where challenges are met with strength and optimism.

Encouraging Mindfulness in the Workplace

Mindfulness in the workplace goes beyond individual practices; it involves creating a collective environment where mindfulness is part of the organization's daily rhythm. Arts leaders can play a critical role in normalizing and promoting mindfulness throughout the team, encouraging practices that help everyone stay present, focused, and connected.

> Start Meetings with a Moment of Silence: Begin each team meeting with a brief moment of silence or a mindfulness exercise, such as deep breathing or guided meditation. This practice helps everyone to ground themselves, clear their minds of distractions, and focus on the purpose of the meeting. It also fosters a sense of calm and presence, setting a positive tone for collaboration and discussion.
>
> Offer Mindfulness Training and Resources: Provide opportunities for staff to learn about mindfulness and develop their own practices. This could include hosting workshops, bringing in mindfulness coaches, or offering access to online courses or apps. Encourage staff to explore different mindfulness techniques, such as meditation, mindful movement, or gratitude practices, and provide time and space for them to practice during the workday.
>
> Create Spaces for Reflection and Relaxation: Designate areas within the workplace where staff can take breaks, reflect, or engage in mindfulness practices. This could be a quiet room with comfortable seating, soothing decor, and calming

music, or simply a corner with plants and soft lighting. Encourage staff to use these spaces to pause, recharge, and return to their work with renewed focus and energy.

<u>Integrate Mindfulness into Everyday Interactions</u>: Encourage mindful communication in daily interactions by promoting practices such as active listening, empathy, and non-judgmental awareness. When engaging with team members, practice being fully present, maintaining eye contact, and genuinely listening to their ideas and concerns. This approach fosters trust, respect, and collaboration, creating a more supportive and cohesive team dynamic.

Promoting Work-Life Balance

A healthy work-life balance is essential for sustaining creativity and preventing burnout. When team members feel overwhelmed or overextended, their capacity for innovation and effective collaboration diminishes. Arts leaders can promote work-life balance by implementing policies and practices that prioritize mental health and well-being and by modeling these behaviors themselves.

<u>Flexible Working Hours and Remote Work Options</u>: Recognize that each team member has unique personal needs and responsibilities. Offer flexible working hours or remote work options to accommodate diverse lifestyles and promote a healthier balance between work and personal life.

Flexible work arrangements can reduce stress, increase job satisfaction, and enhance productivity by allowing staff to work in ways that align with their individual rhythms and needs.

Encourage Regular Breaks and Time Off: Encourage staff to take regular breaks throughout the day to rest and recharge. Promote the importance of taking time off, whether for vacation, mental health days, or simply stepping away from work for a few moments. Ensure that taking time off is normalized and supported, without guilt or pressure. As a leader, demonstrate this by taking breaks yourself and respecting others' need for downtime.

Implement Policies That Prioritize Well-Being: Develop policies that explicitly prioritize mental health and well-being. This could include offering mental health resources, such as counseling or access to wellness programs, providing opportunities for professional development on topics like stress management and resilience, and establishing clear guidelines for work hours and communication to prevent overwork.

Lead by Example: As an arts leader, your behavior sets the tone for the organization. Model a healthy work-life balance by setting boundaries, avoiding excessive overtime, and showing respect for personal time. Share your own practices for managing stress and maintaining balance, and encourage your team to do the same. By leading with authenticity and self-care, you inspire your team to prioritize their own well-being.

Building Emotional Resilience in Teams

Emotional resilience is the capacity to cope with adversity, adapt to change, and maintain a positive outlook, even in challenging situations. In the arts, where uncertainty, rejection, and creative tension are common, building emotional resilience is key to sustaining a motivated and engaged team. Arts leaders can foster emotional resilience by creating a supportive, open, and inclusive environment.

> Foster a Culture of Open Communication: Encourage open dialogue and transparency within your team. Create safe spaces for team members to express their feelings, share their concerns, and offer feedback without fear of judgment or reprisal. Regularly check in with your team to gauge their well-being, and be open to listening and responding with empathy. When team members feel heard and supported, they are more likely to remain resilient in the face of challenges.
>
> Provide Constructive Feedback: Deliver feedback in a way that is supportive, constructive, and focused on growth. Use feedback as an opportunity to celebrate strengths, identify areas for improvement, and inspire development. Frame feedback in terms of specific actions and outcomes, and avoid making it

personal or overly critical. Encourage a growth mindset, where mistakes are seen as learning opportunities rather than failures.

Celebrate Achievements and Progress: Recognize and celebrate the achievements of your team, both big and small. Acknowledge the hard work, creativity, and dedication of each team member, and express gratitude for their contributions. Regularly celebrate milestones, successes, and efforts, creating a positive and uplifting atmosphere that boosts morale and encourages resilience. Celebrating achievements also fosters a sense of belonging and shared purpose, helping to build a stronger and more cohesive team.

Encourage Peer Support and Collaboration: Promote peer support and collaboration by creating opportunities for team members to work together, share ideas, and learn from each other. Encourage mentorship, buddy systems, or peer feedback sessions where team members can offer support and guidance to one another. This collaborative approach fosters a sense of community, strengthens bonds, and builds collective resilience.

Creating a Lasting Impact Through Mindful and Creative Team Culture

Fostering a mindful and creative team culture is about more than just implementing policies or practices; it's about cultivating an environment where every individual feels valued, supported, and empowered to do their best work. When arts leaders prioritize mindfulness, work-life balance, and emotional resilience, they create a culture that nurtures creativity, fosters collaboration, and builds the capacity to thrive in the face of challenges.

By encouraging mindfulness in the workplace, promoting a healthy work-life balance, and building emotional resilience, you help your team navigate the complexities of the arts with grace and strength. As a result, your organization will be better equipped to achieve its creative vision, foster innovation, and make a lasting impact in the community it serves.

Remember, a mindful and creative team culture begins with leadership. As an arts leader, your commitment to these principles can transform the way your team works, collaborates, and grows. By creating a culture of mindfulness and well-being, you lay the foundation for a more inspired, engaged, and resilient organization.

CHAPTER 5

THE IMPACT OF MINDFUL LEADERSHIP ON PERFORMANCE

Balancing Creativity and Performance

Mindful leadership is a powerful approach that extends beyond enhancing individual well-being; it directly influences organizational performance and effectiveness. In the arts, where creativity and innovation are at the heart of every endeavor, mindful leadership fosters an environment where these qualities can flourish. When leaders practice mindfulness, they are more present, self-aware, and emotionally intelligent, which leads to better decision-making, more effective communication, and a stronger, more cohesive team.

Mindfulness helps leaders strike the delicate balance between encouraging creative exploration and maintaining a high level of performance. This balance is critical in the arts, where the pressure to produce impactful work often coexists with the need for innovation and experimentation. By cultivating mindfulness, leaders can create a culture where creativity and performance are not at odds but rather complement and enhance each other.

Enhancing Decision-Making and Problem-Solving

Decision-making and problem-solving are at the core of effective leadership. In the dynamic and unpredictable world of the arts, leaders often face complex challenges that require quick, yet thoughtful decisions. Mindful leaders are better equipped to navigate these complexities because they approach problems with a calm, focused, and open mindset.

> <u>Improved Critical Thinking</u>: Mindfulness encourages leaders to pause and reflect before making decisions, which allows for deeper critical thinking. By being fully present and aware, mindful leaders are less likely to make impulsive decisions driven by stress or anxiety. Instead, they can evaluate situations more thoroughly, consider multiple perspectives, and weigh the potential outcomes. This thoughtful approach leads to more balanced and well-considered decisions that align with both short-term needs and long-term goals.
>
> <u>Enhanced Problem-Solving Skills</u>: Mindfulness practices, such as meditation and reflection, help leaders develop greater cognitive flexibility, which is essential for effective problem-solving. By fostering an open and curious mindset, mindfulness enables leaders to explore various solutions, think creatively, and adapt to changing circumstances. Mindful

leaders are more likely to approach problems with a solution-oriented mindset, viewing challenges as opportunities for growth rather than obstacles.

Navigating Complex Situations with Confidence and Clarity: Mindfulness allows leaders to remain calm and focused, even in high-pressure situations. By cultivating a sense of inner stability, mindful leaders can better manage stress and uncertainty, enabling them to make decisions with greater confidence and clarity. They are less likely to be swayed by external pressures or emotional reactions and are more adept at guiding their teams through complex and ambiguous circumstances.

Boosting Creativity and Innovation

Creativity and innovation are the lifeblood of arts organizations, and mindful leadership plays a pivotal role in fostering an environment where these qualities can thrive. When leaders are mindful, they create a culture where team members feel safe, supported, and valued—conditions that are essential for creative thinking and experimentation.

Encouraging Risk-Taking: Creativity often involves taking risks, trying new approaches, and stepping into the unknown. Mindful leaders understand the importance of creating a psychological safety net for their team, where taking risks is not only accepted but encouraged. By fostering an atmosphere where mistakes are viewed as part of the learning process rather than failures, leaders empower their teams to experiment, innovate, and push the boundaries of their creative potential.

Embracing Failure as a Learning Opportunity: In a mindful organization, failure is not feared but seen as an invaluable source of learning and growth. Mindful leaders model this attitude by openly discussing their own mistakes, reflecting on lessons learned, and encouraging their teams to do the same. This approach reduces the fear of failure and encourages a culture of continuous improvement and innovation.

Creating Space for Exploration and Experimentation: Mindful leaders recognize the importance of creating time and space for creative exploration. They prioritize opportunities for their teams to brainstorm, play, and experiment without the immediate pressure of deadlines or outcomes. This might involve setting aside dedicated time for creative sessions, providing resources for new projects, or encouraging cross-disciplinary collaborations. By fostering an environment where creativity is nurtured, mindful leaders enable their teams to generate fresh ideas, explore new possibilities, and innovate more effectively.

Improving Communication and Collaboration

Effective communication is a hallmark of mindful leadership. In the arts, where collaboration and teamwork are vital to success, leaders who practice mindful communication can build stronger relationships, resolve conflicts more effectively, and create a more inclusive and collaborative team dynamic.

>Active Listening: Mindful leaders practice active listening, a technique that involves fully focusing on the speaker, understanding their message, and responding thoughtfully. Active listening helps leaders build trust and rapport with their team members, ensuring that everyone feels heard and valued. By paying close attention to both verbal and nonverbal cues, leaders can gain deeper insights into their team's needs, concerns, and ideas, fostering a more open and productive dialogue.

>Empathy: Empathy is the ability to understand and share the feelings of others, and it is a critical component of mindful leadership. Mindful leaders practice empathy by being present, compassionate, and nonjudgmental in their interactions with team members. This empathetic approach helps leaders build stronger, more authentic connections with their teams, creating a culture of mutual respect and support. When team members feel understood and appreciated, they are more likely to collaborate effectively, share ideas openly, and work together toward common goals.

> Nonviolent Communication: Nonviolent communication (NVC) is a communication approach that focuses on expressing needs and feelings honestly while listening to others with empathy and understanding. For arts leaders, NVC can be a powerful tool for resolving conflicts and fostering a collaborative team environment. By practicing NVC, leaders can navigate difficult conversations with care, reduce misunderstandings, and build a culture of trust and cooperation. This communication style helps create an inclusive atmosphere where all voices are heard and respected, enhancing team cohesion and collaboration.

The Ripple Effect of Mindful Leadership on Organizational Performance

Mindful leadership has a profound impact on organizational performance. When leaders are mindful, they create a positive ripple effect throughout the organization, influencing not only their own behavior but also the culture, morale, and productivity of their teams.

> Higher Employee Engagement and Retention: Mindful leaders cultivate a work environment where employees feel valued, motivated, and engaged. When team members feel supported and empowered, they are more likely to be committed to their work and remain loyal to the organization. This increased engagement leads to higher levels of productivity, creativity, and overall performance. Additionally,

organizations with mindful leaders often experience lower turnover rates, as employees are more satisfied with their work environment and feel a stronger sense of purpose and belonging.

Greater Innovation and Competitive Advantage: A culture of mindfulness fosters creativity and innovation, giving arts organizations a competitive edge in a rapidly changing landscape. When leaders encourage experimentation, embrace diverse perspectives, and support creative risk-taking, they enable their teams to develop new ideas, adapt to challenges, and stay ahead of industry trends. This continuous innovation is critical for maintaining relevance and achieving long-term success.

Improved Organizational Resilience: Mindful leadership enhances organizational resilience by building a culture that is flexible, adaptive, and prepared for change. Mindful leaders are more attuned to the emotional needs of their teams and can respond to crises or setbacks with calm and clarity. They are also better equipped to anticipate and navigate challenges, ensuring that the organization can weather disruptions and emerge stronger on the other side.

Leading with Mindfulness for Peak Performance

Mindful leadership is a transformative approach that not only enhances individual well-being but also drives organizational performance. By fostering mindfulness in decision-making, creativity, communication, and collaboration, arts leaders can create a thriving environment where both creativity and performance flourish.

Through mindfulness, leaders can balance the pursuit of artistic excellence with the well-being of their teams, fostering a culture that supports both innovation and sustained success. The impact of mindful leadership extends beyond the individual leader; it permeates the entire organization, leading to higher engagement, greater innovation, and a more resilient and adaptive organization.

Embracing mindful leadership is an invitation to reimagine what is possible in the arts, creating a future where creativity and performance are not mutually exclusive but are deeply intertwined, driving organizations toward new heights of impact and achievement.

CHAPTER 6

INTEGRATING MINDFULNESS INTO ORGANIZATIONAL STRATEGY

Mindfulness as a Strategic Priority

For arts organizations to truly embrace mindful leadership, mindfulness must be integrated into the very core of the organization's strategy. This means going beyond implementing a few mindfulness practices or initiatives; it requires embedding mindfulness as a fundamental value that informs every decision, policy, and action. By doing so, arts leaders can foster a more innovative, resilient, and sustainable organization that thrives not only creatively but also in terms of well-being and community impact.

This chapter provides a roadmap for how arts leaders can weave mindfulness into their organizational strategy, ensuring that it becomes a continuous and evolving priority. It explores ways to align mindfulness with mission and vision statements, strategic planning, and organizational policies, and offers practical advice for measuring the impact of these efforts and sustaining a mindful culture over time.

Embedding Mindfulness in Mission and Vision Statements

The foundation of any organization's strategy is its mission and vision statements. These guiding principles articulate the purpose, direction, and values of the organization. To create a mindful organization, it is essential to align these statements with the principles of mindfulness, empathy, and well-being.

> Reflecting on Core Values: Begin by reflecting on your current mission and vision statements. Do they explicitly convey a commitment to mindfulness, compassion, creativity, and holistic well-being? If not, consider revising these statements to better reflect these values. For example, you might incorporate language that emphasizes the importance of creating a nurturing environment for artists and staff, fostering emotional intelligence, or promoting community engagement through mindful practices.
>
> Communicating Mindfulness to Stakeholders: By embedding mindfulness into your mission and vision, you signal its importance to all stakeholders—staff, artists, audiences, and funders. This alignment sets a clear expectation that mindfulness is a core organizational value, encouraging everyone involved with your organization to embrace and support this focus.
>
> Aligning Goals and Actions with Mindfulness Principles: Ensure that your organizational goals and

actions align with your revised mission and vision statements. For instance, if your mission now includes a commitment to fostering a mindful and compassionate environment, consider how this can be reflected in your hiring practices, programming decisions, and community partnerships.

Mindful Strategic Planning

Strategic planning is a critical process for setting an organization's direction and priorities. By integrating mindfulness into strategic planning, arts leaders can make more intentional, thoughtful decisions that support both the creative and operational health of the organization.

> <u>Mindfulness Exercises for Strategic Sessions</u>: Begin strategic planning sessions with mindfulness exercises to help participants focus, connect, and engage more deeply in the process. Simple practices like guided breathing, body scans, or moments of silence can help everyone become present and centered, fostering a more collaborative and reflective atmosphere.
>
> <u>Reflective Questions and Open Dialogue</u>: Use reflective questions to explore how mindfulness can shape your organizational goals, priorities, and strategies for growth. Questions such as "How can we foster a culture of mindfulness within our team?" or "What role does mindfulness play in achieving our mission?" encourage open dialogue and creative

thinking. This approach ensures that strategic decisions are grounded in your core values and aligned with the well-being of your team and community.

<u>Integrating Mindfulness into Decision-Making</u>: Incorporate mindfulness into the decision-making process by encouraging leaders and team members to pause, reflect, and consider multiple perspectives before making choices. This practice helps reduce impulsive decisions driven by stress or bias, leading to more thoughtful and balanced outcomes that benefit the entire organization.

Creating Mindful Policies and Practices

To sustain a mindful culture, arts organizations must develop policies and practices that support mindfulness and well-being at all levels. This involves creating an environment where mindfulness is not just encouraged but actively supported through everyday actions and organizational norms.

<u>Guidelines for Mindful Communication</u>: Develop guidelines that promote mindful communication within your organization. Encourage practices such as active listening, respectful dialogue, and empathy. Train staff on nonviolent communication techniques that help resolve conflicts constructively and build trust and collaboration among team members.

Protocols for Conflict Resolution: Establish protocols for conflict resolution that prioritize empathy, understanding, and mindfulness. This could include mediation practices, regular check-ins, or structured dialogues that allow all parties to express their feelings and perspectives in a safe and supportive environment.

Flexible Work Arrangements and Mental Health Support: Implement policies that support work-life balance and mental health, such as flexible work arrangements, remote work options, or mental health days. Provide access to mental health resources, such as counseling or wellness programs, and offer regular wellness check-ins to ensure that staff feel supported and valued.

Regular Wellness Initiatives: Incorporate mindfulness into organizational routines through regular wellness initiatives like mindfulness workshops, yoga sessions, meditation breaks, or team-building activities that emphasize well-being. These initiatives help embed mindfulness into the daily rhythm of the organization, reinforcing its importance and impact.

Measuring the Impact of Mindfulness

To ensure that mindfulness becomes an integral part of your organizational strategy, it is essential to measure its impact. This involves defining success in mindful terms, gathering feedback, and celebrating achievements to maintain momentum and engagement.

> Defining Success in Mindful Terms: Traditional metrics such as financial performance and audience numbers remain important, but they should be complemented by indicators that reflect your commitment to mindfulness. Develop key performance indicators (KPIs) that capture dimensions like employee well-being, team cohesion, and creative innovation. For example, you might track staff retention rates, levels of reported job satisfaction, the frequency of mindfulness practices, or the diversity and inclusivity of your programming.
>
> Creating Feedback Loops: Establish regular feedback loops that allow your team and stakeholders to share their experiences with mindfulness practices in the organization. Use surveys, focus groups, and informal discussions to gather insights on how mindfulness is impacting team dynamics, decision-making, and overall well-being. This feedback will help you refine your approach, identify areas for improvement, and adapt your strategies to better support a mindful culture.
>
> Celebrating Mindful Achievements: Acknowledge and celebrate the achievements and milestones of your organization's journey toward mindfulness. Recognize staff members who embody mindful leadership, share success stories that highlight the

impact of mindfulness on your work, and create opportunities for reflection and gratitude. Celebrating these achievements helps reinforce the importance of mindfulness and encourages ongoing commitment to this transformative approach.

Sustaining a Mindful Organization

Sustaining mindfulness as a core value requires ongoing effort and engagement. It is not a destination but a continuous practice that evolves with the organization's growth and changing needs.

> Mindfulness as a Continuous Practice: Recognize that mindfulness is a journey, not a one-time initiative. Encourage a mindset of growth and learning where mindfulness is seen as an ongoing practice rather than a fixed goal. Create opportunities for regular training, workshops, and retreats that deepen the understanding and practice of mindfulness across all levels of the organization. Regularly revisit and revise your mindfulness practices to ensure they remain relevant and impactful.
>
> Engaging Stakeholders in Your Mindful Journey: Mindfulness should not be confined to your organization's internal team; it should extend to all stakeholders, including artists, community members, funders, and partners. Share your vision and progress openly, and invite stakeholders to participate in mindfulness initiatives. Consider

offering mindfulness training or workshops to community members, artists, or partner organizations, creating a ripple effect that extends your impact beyond your immediate team.

<u>Adapting to Change with Mindfulness</u>: In an ever-changing world, mindfulness can help your organization remain flexible, resilient, and adaptive. Develop a mindful approach to change management where transitions are handled with empathy, transparency, and thoughtful communication. Use mindfulness practices to help your team navigate uncertainty, manage stress, and maintain focus during periods of change or challenge. Encourage your team to view change not as a threat but as an opportunity for growth and learning.

Building a Mindful Organization for the Future

Integrating mindfulness into your organizational strategy is a powerful way to enhance creativity, resilience, and performance. By embedding mindfulness into your mission and vision, strategic planning, and daily practices, you create an environment where well-being and innovation thrive together.

Mindfulness is not just a tool for managing stress or enhancing focus; it is a transformative approach that can fundamentally reshape how your organization operates and impacts the world. By committing to mindfulness as a strategic priority, you foster a culture of empathy, openness, and creativity that empowers your team to reach its full potential.

As you continue on this mindful journey, remember that every step—no matter how small—brings you closer to a more balanced, inclusive, and sustainable future for your organization and the communities you serve. Embrace mindfulness as a core value, and watch as it transforms not only your leadership but also the very fabric of your organization.

ABOUT THE AUTHOR

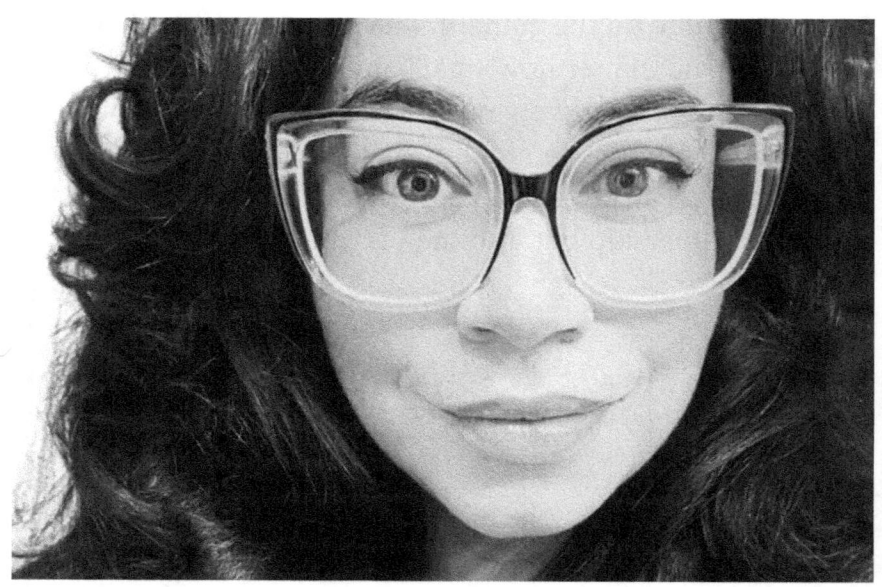

Denise Zubizarreta is a neurodivergent mixed media interdisciplinary artist and Cultural Operations Specialist of Puerto Rican and Cuban descent, with decades of experience in various creative fields. She is currently an arts and culture writer for multiple leading publications that offer curated and critical perspectives on contemporary art, film, television, and culture.

Zubizarreta holds a B.F.A. in Fine Art from Rocky Mountain College of Art + Design, and is completing her Master's in Arts Leadership and Cultural Management (M.A.L.C.M.) at Colorado State University. Her passion for arts and culture drives her to explore and challenge the intersections of post-colonial theory, identity, technology and traditions in her writing and mixed media works.

www.ingramcontent.com/pod-product-compliance
Lightning Source LLC
Chambersburg PA
CBHW070417230526
45471CB00006B/2852